CASHING CHECKS WITH JIM MORRISON

Praise for
CASHING CHECKS WITH JIM MORRISON

✳ ✳ ✳

"*CASHING CHECKS with Jim Morrison* offers a surreal cascade of archetypes from, among others, ancient Greece, the Bible, American Literature, and pop culture. Moving through it is the speaker's companion spirit and guru, Jim Morrison—Lizard King, Narcissus/Adonis. Set in a world where, in Albert Einstein's words, 'reality is merely an illusion,' Lindsey Martin-Bowen's poems are alive with wit, evocative imagery, insight, and sometimes downright playfulness. Through heeding Morrison's counsel to 'go weirder,' she's made this collection reader-friendly."

—WILLIAM TROWBRIDGE, Missouri Poet Laureate, 2012-2016
Author, *Call Me Fool* (2022)

✳ ✳ ✳

"In Lindsey Martin-Bowen's *CASHING CHECKS with Jim Morrison*, I relish every word, compelled by the poet's stories and singing voice. Fantasy and fact merge in these invocations of the seminal American rocker Morrison and of his spirit. Join me as a reader in exploring this exciting testament to the power of language to resurrect history and wonder."

—DENISE LOW, Kansas Poet Laureate, 2007–2009
Poetry Unbound Featured Poet

✳ ✳ ✳

Also by Lindsey Martin-Bowen

POETRY

The BOOK of FRENZIES
(Pierian Springs Press 2022)

Where Water Meets the Rock
(39 WEST PRESS 2017)

CROSSING KANSAS with Jim Morrison
(Paladin Contemporaries 2016)

Inside Virgil's Garage
(Chatter House Press 2013)

Standing on the Edge of the World
(Woodley Press/Washburn University 2008)

Second Touch
(Chapbook 1990)

FICTION

Rapture Redux: A Comedy
(Paladin Contemporaries 2014)

Hamburger Haven
(Paladin Contemporaries 2009)

Cicada Grove
(Paladin Contemporaries 1992)

redbat books
pacific northwest
writers series

CASHING CHECKS
with Jim Morrison

poems

LINDSEY MARTIN-BOWEN

redbat
books

redbat books
La Grande, Oregon
2023

Printed in the United States of America

First Edition: October 2023

Trade Paperback ISBN: 978-1-946970-09-1

Library of Congress Control Number: 2023945755

Published by
redbat books
La Grande, OR 97850
www.redbatbooks.com

Text set in Calluna

Author photo by Nelli Sudbrock

Cover painting:
"Indian appears in Mountains South of Cortez across from Sleeping Ute Mountain" by Lindsey Martin-Bowen
Acrylic, 29.5" x 23.5"

Book design by
Kristin Summers, redbat design | www.redbatdesign.com

TABLE OF CONTENTS

For Robert "Bob" Haynes, mentor and lifetime friend,
who often gave me "shelter from the storm."

BACK STORY

Years ago, when I screamed down asphalt through mauve Kansas fields
and the Flint Hills, rock shaman Jim Morrison crawled out of my car
stereo while a yellow hornet on the windshield danced like a Kachina
in a sand painting. It was magic. Perhaps. I still don't know.
Jim came with me to find La Loba*, in hopes she'd resurrect his bones.

But the wolf woman left him alone, and I led him back to Paris
and the Père-Lachaise Cemetery. There, Jim's dark monument, wrought
with graffiti, commemorates him. I'd thought this story had ended.
But I was wrong. He won't leave me alone. He pushes into poems
and ignoring his resurrection, into this collection—joining figures

from everywhere—ancient Greece and Eleusinian mysteries, wild
and wooly creatures in the frenzies, and post-modern philosophers.
Even today, he whispers to me when I stare at a waffled, red-lace sky
filled with popcorn clouds looming above our foothills on this New
Year's Day when the Vienna Philharmonic Orchestra plays a Strauss waltz

designed with Mid-eastern chords for Zeitgeist 1865—100 years before Jim
played live on Ed Sullivan's show. A dancer in the Vienna show ogles
a ballerina, stalks her in palace halls. I hear her sobs echo off of ornate
archways where angels bow to Jesus Christ who cannot hear her screams
above the cymbals and kettle drums. I do and pour ashes over my head.

---

*Wolf woman. Bone woman. According to Southwest legends
(from various tribes and Mexican cultures), La Loba works with angels
to gather bones of humans and wolves, then resurrect them.

ELEGIES for a BROKEN WORLD

Jim Says I Must "Dig Deeper"
when I Write—"Expose Myself
to My Deepest Fears."

These Poems Are My Replies.

AFTER READING "SAUDADE" by Erika L. Sánchez

You say you live in the Republic of Flowers.
I live in the Republic of Broccoli,
where I learn to fry skirts with frilly
words that mean everything
to those awake during wee hours,
scrubbing blood off floors or walls
after vampires break mirrors
that reflect too much sun.
I cannot bow to the authority
of flowers. I must bow
to the authority of vegetables,
or I'll become vulnerable as Mary Lu,
the girl local roofers raped inside a pool hall,
where they spread her like Indian Paintbrush
plucked from tundra surrounding
a mountain town. There, contractors,
carpenters, and workmen keep women
locked inside bedrooms.
      I need to survive in the city.
I'm scared when I inhale
scents from moldy limestone walls
circling Chicago or Miami,
wherever immigrants enter,
and the Man jots their names
onto lists he sends to the Asp
who executes them before they commit
crimes or marry citizens who turn them
into parts of us as we stroll
between two lions at the edge of a lagoon,
where swans circle each other
then dip into green water
and perform for the peacocks
on the shore, as if this were before
the second World War—
before Europe shivered
with news from Germany—
that second fall from grace.

ANTIGONE'S RANT
(What I'd Give)

I'd give a three-headed dog
and Charon rowing
through the Styx.

I'd give the blood of a tulip,
a cracked cup,

and bellies of black
clouds festering.

I'd give a ride on Chiron,
a dead barge,
or a stampede of Centaurs.

I'd give the morning shadows,
asps in the desert,

And I would give
my burning lips.

SELF-PORTRAIT
as BATHSHEBA

A little rest is all I want—
here, on a red clay roof.
Wisps of wind twist
my hair into knots,
and lavender
scents relax me.
Bathing away from
tight, steamy rooms
heightens my mood.

I don't invite him in.
After he sees me nude,
he calls me to him.
He's the king ruling
my husband and me,
so I cannot say no.
Tonight, he knows
I'm alone—he sent Uriah
to the forefront of a siege.

Now, I face metal, Janus
skies with pains in my womb.
Pinched nerves tell me
this life within will last
outside but a few days:
God's vengeance on the king.
But me? I merely want peace:
No interest in conspiracies,
No plans to start a dynasty.

PERSEPHONE WAITS
at the HADES INTERSECTION

Each fall, he drags me here,
pulls me away from perfumed
pillows, sunlit rooms,
and city lights that flicker
not far from my window.

I miss strolling to the market,
where I finger pomegranates—
sipping coffee in a café,
and munching baklava
at afternoon tea.

Here, traffic shoves me to the curb,
splashes me with black water.
I wheel over asphalt, dodge semis
and SUVS, while I'm locked
inside a hot metal box.

SELF-PORTRAIT
in Cracked Mirror

A bit of *Guernica*—
my mother's nightmare.
Thick, black kohl
outlines eyes.
One stares left,
the other, right,
and hair twists into
boa tongues winding
here and everywhere—
a Gorgon's headdress.
Shoulders twitch—
wasps on a window ledge.

BEATNIK NIGHT in BALDWIN CITY, KANSAS
(*Channeling Jim Morrison*)

for Denise Low-Weso

They're all here—those hip ghosts from the past,
Burroughs, Waldrum, Ginsberg, Kerouac—
Ferlinghetti's riding a Ferris
wheel behind the City Library,
where everyone's in black, fingers snap
Bohemian drumbeats, and bongos

back up poetry readings ranging
from whispers to shouts and the rhythm
of sticks beating hard as blood pulsing
through arteries after tough swimming
in the Y on a February
day, icy with charcoal smells, when

berets on ears fail to keep them warm.
It's still a cool way to brave the storm.

INSPIRED, in part,
by TWO INCIDENTS

The killer brought *In Cold Blood*
with him to the therapy group
because he heard a new Yale study
says people who read novels
each day may live years
longer than those who don't.
Thirty minutes a day of *Jane Eyre*
can take away the quick death
magazine features and newspaper
stories sometimes bring.

I lift my eyes from *Gardens
in the Dunes*, Silko's novel,
and stare at the eagle's shadow
hovering on the horizon
the very moment the Dakotas
at Standing Rock demonstrate
to stop oil pipelines.
Still, I'm unsure if the killer's
capital punishment sentence
will be waived.

NO EXIT

(with apologies to John-Paul Sartre)

Hell is other people, you say. Sometimes I agree,
      like tonight, when I want to fly
          through the Rocky Mountains,
             head east across the Atlantic,
               land in the Alps awhile

and return through the San Juan Range
               where a rugged snow,
                 a thick, rocky snow
might keep me cabin-bound a few days.

Yet here, light snow dusting the foothills
        creeps in at night
           through these hills encasing us in La Grande,
             and it clings to the city at dawn
And in the halcyon late mornings
     after the sleet burns off,
        when the sun splashes houses
              with the snow melt of Cove
         and the sharp shadows of our small city
           make the town look like
             it had just been painted.

Then the wind comes up at four o'clock
             and scours the hills
And the veil of white in early evening.
        And then comes another flurry
          when the new night snow
        drifts in,
   And in that veil of crystals, we sleep, locked-in,
         snuggled against the hills.

RELATIVITY LESSON

to my granddaughter, Ashe Veronica

You take one of my wrists,
unfold it, finger veins
protruding on the forearm.
"What are these?" you ask.
"Veins," I say. "They carry blood
back to the heart, and they pick up
oxygen there. Blood needs that."
You shake your head. "No," you say.
"That means you're old."

You seem to catch my forced smile
when I snap, "I won't be old till
I'm one-hundred. Then, you'll be
as old as your mom is now."
Your face becomes a question—
furrowed eyebrows, a slight frown,
as if you realize you aren't immune
to this universal state,
at least, on this planet.

> *Footnote:*
> *When I see Ashe a week later,*
> *she tells me, "You're beautiful."*
> *"You are, too," I reply.*
> *She entwines her fingers and smiles.*
> *We say nothing but know.*

ASHE'S PEOPLE

for Ki Russell

Balloon faces
on stringy bodies—
Not usual stick figures,
their long, lean limbs
stretch down the page,
morphing her people
into tall wild flowers
blooming in meadows.
They pop-up in all colors.
I wonder if Ashe
has tapped into a
genetic, Native style.

We stem from Montauks,
Granddaughter Ashe
and me, our long, wild
hair, free-flowing back
many generations.
We weren't forced
onto reservations.
Yet we endured that
trail of tears during
our Oregon migration—
imprisoned still by
White Man's lies.

DAY of the DEAD
in the Season of the Corona

No one listens anymore.
No one works in tandem.
No oxen pull this cart.
Trembling now, it falls apart.

It's the day, it's the day—
O yes, it's the holy day—
it's the Day of the Dead.

The center hub's blown, exploded.
Rioting in city squares—
rioting along beaches:
Is this anarchy—or a greater horror?

The blood of children rushes onto shores.
Innocents no more, their lungs fill
till they can't speak—can't breathe.

Their passions now senseless, uneasy—
bringing the strange revelation:
Some Second Coming lies on the horizon.

A wide-winged beast rises above—
eyes black and gleaming, onyx
glistening through bone.

Oh Momma, Momma,
come back, come back
again. This world's too cold.

No lion-bodied beast slouches
toward Bethlehem. It's one
with a jackal's head, a jackal's soul.

QUANTUM MECHANICAL LOVE

for Jenny Lorraine Nielsen

> *Bell's (physics) theorem: Particles of light may be so*
> *intimately linked that a change to one affects the other,*
> *even when they are far apart.*
> —John Bell, 1964

Entanglement, John Bell called it:
love at the speed of light.
Light-years apart, our particles dance,
move arms and legs in two-steps
to the same beat—interplanetary music.

Here, on this shore in another galaxy,
Jim Morrison and I are fire, ash, and air.
Our energy hovers above sunlit land.
Our bodies sink into iridescent sand.
Sunhats above brows almost hide
the panic tangoing on our faces.

If nothing is certain until it happens,
this probability holds:
when Jesus and others rise to Heaven,
into that stardust dimension, a silver string
connects them to those they love.

SELF-PORTRAIT
as Second Wife

The ghost in the cupboards
won't leave me alone.
She rattles her teacups—
Havilland, a German import.
They clink in time to her garden
chimes during a quick,
summer wind.

The specter lures me
to a wall that smells scorched.
I see a kettle left on a burner,
remnants of ash, pillars of smoke.
There, on a shelf, the teapot
reflects charred doors,
a night blazing.

Now the room's cold, and
her fingers run icy rivulets
across my shoulders.
Dashing across the room,
she morphs into a comet,
then turns into thick, white haze
that lingers above her dahlias.

The morning sunlight turns
the blooms into flames, reminding
me her image won't fade—
her incense, patchouli, pierced navel,
and purple hair. And she avers
my road to God is wrong—
or a relative thing, this truth.

KOHL-RIMMED EYES

Upon viewing a model of an ancient Egyptian boat with oar-men

I remember them—those, black, kohl-edged eyes.
I painted them on people I sculpted from clay
those days when teachers let us play to learn.

My statues didn't row a funerary boat with
Egyptians looking distracted as if oaring
halfway between sleep and dreaming.

I grew and forgot them until kohl-rimmed eyes
re-appeared on some of my students. Mideast
girls at the university painted them on eyelids

to emphasize their black, fluid eyes. Then,
one night, hundreds of black-rimmed eyes
formed kaleidoscopes festooning my walls.

They landed there during a sleepless night
when Uncle Liam almost died, pole piercing
his chest, like a stake through a vampire's heart.

But the eye prisms didn't see that. Glazed
over, they stared at me instead—cut into my chest.
Sometimes, they still sneak into my dreams.

I HEAR AMERICA MELTING

*for Kamal E. Kimball (after
"I Hear America Rusting")*

It sizzles on each coastline—
frying from fluorescent lights
that pollute nights. It keeps us
from the solace of star-gazing,
at perhaps Orion, Cepheus,
and Cassiopeia.
They blur the stratosphere.
Many here still dream
of a melting pot,
but ours is boiling over, lost
in a radiated plot somewhere
south of Santa Fe,
where some say aliens
landed. Perhaps they, too,
want to melt into our
populace, become pod-people,
like those in a 1990s
TV show, to merge into dreams
of interplanetary peace,
while we feast from a Vegan menu
of tofu turkey, black beans,
peas, and maybe, *kale.*
And now, the sounds boom
louder—auto backfires,
gunshots from pistols
and sometimes,
AR-15s—sounds more akin
to a meltdown than
to any holy merger.

ALONG the CURB

to Michelle Boisseau (after "Flesh is Air Too")

In Amsterdam, you
floated along a canal
where you saw Donald
Barthelme sip wine. Faces
from ghostly millennia

morphed into bubbles—
universes I can't see
from this earthy spot,
stuck beside a cracked sidewalk,
earth-bound for many seasons.

Under those bubbles,
eons of days pass, and I
kick leaves, clustering
at a corner and clinging
to grates to avoid their fates,

while I dream of Dutch
scenes, Dublin streets, and James Joyce
strolling them at night.
Perhaps I'll hear Donald, or
Sylvia and Anne gabbing.

Your face still lingers
above a shoreline, in photos
of Greek isles, where you
wander among the Gorgons.
I stumble along the curb.

MIRROR IMAGES

with apologies to William Stafford

1

Harsh light filters through blinds
into your room, where a mirror
reflects each line in your cheeks
and repeats that detailed,
diligent view of your neck,
as if that mirror would be fined
for missing one crack.

2

You argue it's just the glaring light,
but more and more, you note
those same lines in photos, too.
Each year, in fact, they run
deeper—more rugged cracks—
arroyos in fields, they dig deep
then split into tributaries.

3

Spread open on the coffee table,
a magazine feature boasts
"Middle Age and the Art of Renewal."
You thumb through it, while ice melts
in your glass. Then the glass melts,
disintegrating like sand draining
through an hourglass.

4

Another day passes.
By midnight, your memory
goes blank with loss:
your time, your name.
And then in the darkened
window, you no longer
recognize your face.

NARCISSUS in the OLD FOLKS HOME

He dawdles each morning
in the bathroom—
bending over the sink,
tweezers in hand,
plucking nose hairs
and trimming
his mustache.

One of the girls
told me he nags
the director to install
a mirror over his bed.
And the gardener
tells me the koi fish
in the pond start
twitching after he
stares at the water
for hours each day.

I thought I'd taught him
a lesson eons ago,
but rats like him
just don't get it. And
he gave me a bad rap.
Once my name held honor:
Daughter of Oceanus.
Yet today, "Nemesis"
equates with "enemy"—
all because of him.

HOW YOU DULL the PAIN
UNDER this SILENT CANOPY

to Jim Morrison

In memory of James Tate (December 8, 1943-July 8, 2015)

Sometimes I suffer with it, too, this slow burn
spreading into tributaries in the chest—yet
alcohol's a temporary solution working best

with much dilution—Communion wine,
half water—one sip or two—goes down
far more smoothly, keeps the mind less woozy.

You claim love's mainly pain. I say those who love
us most don't always treat us right. Yet because they
often do, they set us adrift with skewed expectations.

Here, under Caribbean skies, a penguin leads her
brood through tall grasses where cockatiels fly and
alight on branches. The arctic birds dart around

snakes performing deadly dances. They take
jagged steps, toes turned inward, whirling
away from vipers until the birds almost keel.

Most penguins don't dig this hot aquatic scene
with thick palms instead of evergreens under skies
flat as blue paint inside a Victorian canopy for a royal

wedding. And smells of poi and hot spices don't do
their bills justice. They prefer salmon from icy seas,
where they swim and dive deep—far from a glowering sun.

Tonight, they'll try not to stink when they soak their feet
in Epson-salt water, sip a pear drink, and seek out a sailor
to help them find a ball of cheese, the perfect ball of Cheese.

And I wonder if those young birds, like me, will learn
to protect themselves. If they'll glean we're moths drawn to
that which might—at any moment—burst us into flames.

ADONIS in MID-LIFE

His torso's thicker now.
He's taken to eating oats
and trail mix in a peanut
butter concoction his wife
calls "goop." He shies
from cooked broccoli
and carrots, but loves
canned *Le Seur* peas.

And he doesn't work out
at the gym. Too much
pressure there to fit in—
and those steel bars
overhead might swing,
knock him to the floor.
He isn't sure he could
pull himself back up.

A MORTAL LEASH

(After "A Mortal Lease" by Edith Wharton)

Jim and I howl at the moon magnetizing a red-lit sea.
It turns us into senseless lunatics and playthings
for royalty and other gods. Or perhaps, we stay
slaves to elemental laws—circling our masters,
as if they were deities who reign over us.
Awestruck, we watch them, then slip like shadows
into spaces where they peruse newspapers
and share a day of doings that we can't conceive,

like some pinnacle we can't reach, shadows folding
over that gigantic peak lost to those with noses on earth.
We turn noses skyward, eyes set on infinity, then lower
them to the road and dash—so we won't be goaded.
Again, we slip into collars, keep paws on the ground,
and sniff our way home, taking a block for one more round.

OUR FRONT DOOR
in the Time of the Corona

A Christmas wreath still hangs on our door,
and between battles, a tiny nutcracker rests
in prickly needles. His blue jacket with gold epaulets
shows he protects us from the invisible
enemy–a virus swelling to a pandemic.
Tonight, he reminds me of Christmas—children, grand-
children huddled around the table. Ashe in her red smock
looks like an elf & Rook seems too grown-up. Three
Chihuahuas & a Shepherd congregate on woven rugs.
All of us snuggle close—no six-foot social distancing.
You scoffed at me when I warned about the jackal.
Now, he squints from the TV, his onyx eyes glinting
while he sings the Day of the Dead, Dear,
& our fears reappear. They push and shove
each other, trying to trample our threshold.
Though it's April, I don't hang the spring wreath.
Its yellow daffodils, orange lilies, red tulips
& tendrils of vines winding around frail blossoms
no longer tempt me to display its glory.
I won't welcome the world to step inside.

BLACK HIJAB: MY MASK

It came today—the black hijab to wrap
around my nose and mouth.
A magical scarf, it transports me to
Jerusalem before the cobalt twilight,

when leaves fluttering in light winds
urge me to close my eyes to see you,

my City of Dreams. I follow stone streets,
whisk past palm fronds, pines, and fir trees,

and your buff-colored buildings
spreading across an oasis: The Holy Land.

Even in these days of plagues and fear, I ache
to visit you. Black hijab hiding my identity,

I step inside sand-colored towers rising
above clay tile roofs and huge blue domes

curving like cheek-bones or breasts
that feed giant babies. Despite wars

and fires, you stay steady as a loyal lover,
who awaits his wife's return—Hosea

holding on for Gomer and perhaps
the Lord awaiting the Israelites

after they squandered much time,
devotion, and money on gilded idols—

encased in onyx, unlike a black hijab—
no lace, no ruffles, no frills.

JIM SEES HIMSELF in MY POEMS

His curls slide across his forehead
as he thrusts his chin upward and
purses his lips, then licks them.

He laughs and winks. "Those two
without my name—about Narcissus
and Adonis—they're about me, too?"

"Perhaps. Who knows? They may be
about any middle-aged men. Maybe
they aren't about you. You left at age 27."

He shakes his head. "Gods and goddesses
stay within us forever. But they aren't
holy. They're vain, selfish—not saints."

Then he grins, his eyes gleaning with his
Shaman flirtation. "And I'm the Lizard
King—like Narcissus. Or maybe Thor."

FRENZIES and OTHER SURREAL MEANS of ESCAPE

Jim says, "Go Weirder."
And Frenzies Roll in.

"The poet's eye in
a fine frenzy rolling, doth
glance from heaven to
earth . . . gives to airy nothing
a local habitation . . ."

—William Shakespeare
(*A Midsummer Night's Dream*, Vi.12)

CHIHUAHUA CITY

Julio had enough of Great Danes.
So he decided to roll to Old Mexico's
desert and grab a pooch he knew
would appreciate life in the States, especially
after rains came and flooded the doggie
desert. Meanwhile, the Chihuahuas started
worrying about volcanoes and the woes
they'd bring. At any rate, Julio and Bonita
jumped into a jeep, circa '78, so the police
wouldn't likely swipe it. They flew over arroyos
and plains in the Chihuahua state, where they picked
up Charlie the Ape. He raised dogs and rented
out border collies, so he showed them a place
in the hills—the best spot for a Chihuahua haggle.
Looking like aliens with huge black eyes and
narrow cheeks, Chihuahuas sprang out of a creek.
Crawling from sand burrows, others whizzed through
skies, no surprise for Charlie and Julio.
Two tiny dogs shimmy across a log then dashed
to Julio and Bonita. They fed the pups cheese
and peanut butter creams, so the dogs leapt into
the jeep, and all four-wheeled home where
the Chihuahuas now roam Mexican tile floors
and tremble like *piñatas* in wind, never again
to be chased away from the States.

AUDREY the IGUANA

O, such a day it was—
with bright sun, no fog,
after Audrey the Iguana
danced on the staircase all
night long—at least, until the wee
hour before dawn, when two
salamanders delivered three
bottles of milk for morning tea.
Meanwhile, Henry the Crocodile
took off for London after Colonel
P sent roses to Audrey's room.
Just the same, Alfred the D
hit the scene really mean
and begged Audrey for cash.
So Henry returned and rescued
the waif, keeping her safe by
tossing Alfred enough pounds
to marry him to his paramour.
And Freddy the Goon crooned
to Audrey under the streetlamps.
Nevertheless, although all was a mess,
Audrey sang her way to stardom,
no more had to face arrest
by the Bobby at Covington Gardens.

MORE VEGETABLE LINGUISTICS

1

José the Rutabaga was sick of
home-cooking so he opened
a bistro near l'Arc de Triomphe
where he last danced
under the moon in the grooves
between thick mulch, sweet
potatoes, and carrots. He asked Jack
the Beet to join in his feat,
where they could grow thick
skins to protect their soft meats
from beasts and other elements.

2

Simultaneously, Ms. Marie
Broccoli and her mama, Madame
Rene Cauliflower—with her granny
hair coiffure, opened a café inside
Le Louvre. Each morning, they
shimmer with dew during June
and July when morning glories
bloom and climb gates. They
awake early to bake all croissants
before eight, then feel wind against
their heads, while they await
the perfect hour to lie in bed.

3

But *la piece d'resistance*,
appeared in France when Francois
Asparagus opened a restaurant
beside the Eiffel Tower. It
exploded in phallic energy—
stems stretching toward sun,
and Henri Celery grew ridges
between his shoots that lasted
until Sister Elaine Artichoke
spit spiky leaves at the moon.

AN ELEPHANT-LOBSTER'S
SEA GARDEN

Dolby, an elephant-lobster wanted
to drop a few pounds to fit into his tux
for his high school's upcoming prom.
So wearing his silver crown, he dived
deep into the sea—down, down
to his watery garden where red and blue
coral surrounds lobster cousins who
shuttle through black sand and seaweed
waving like ribbons in wind. Dolby grabbed
Cousin Edgar and they hid there, then wiggled
antennae to lure minnows they'd slash
with claws. This diet was perfect, Dolby
knew, especially if a salmon or two swam
through, he'd raise his HDL. Meanwhile,
Edgar got lost while pursuing a jellyfish
who wished he'd never been born.

FOX SOUP II (*at Downton Abbey*)

O they hunted so long—
Lady Mary and Matthew,
trying to tie a tryst like those
in the days when Jane and Liz,
Mr. Darcy, and of course, Mr. Bingley,
came along to that meadow an acre
away from the rose bushes edging
the lawn, where Richardson cornered
the fox who'd been darting left and right,
fighting for his life in the wilderness
called England. Even now, this remains
a pastoral spot, with poplars and oaks
across the lot, far away from London's
Baker Street, long after Sherlock
and John meet and even longer
before anyone conspired to erect
the V&A, where Albert and Victoria
still rest today—yet not all that long
after they filled their bellies
with soup made from a fox.

DUMPSTER DIVING

It was one of those nights when the moon
was so high, it stumbled across the sky,
leaving streaks of light that caused Julio
to sneeze. Meanwhile, Ralph the crocodile
snored in the room next door. Now glassy-eyed,
Julio stared at the ceiling, then at skies outside,
popped over to Ralph's and booted
him to the floor. "Time to cruise," he
said and kicked Ralph again. Then
they hopped into Ralph's red coupe
and headed to Nancy's All-Night Diner,

where Audrey the Iguana hovered,
still in despair that she'd lost her
broad-brimmed hat. She slid to the wall,
to let Julio and Ralph into the stall,
and the three sped through a pot of Joe.
Then, they stared outside, to see a cloud
ride an eagle's shadow on the horizon
the last minutes before sunrise.

DIVE-BOMBING

Morgan the Fly needed a ride
to the rodeo in Pendleton, a
city in eastern Oregon.
So he thumbed one with Evan the Buck,
who drove an oil rig west *en route*
to the Pacific Ocean. Meanwhile, Mack
the Jackalope wanted to smuggle
dope across dry Kansas plains and
avoid oil spills in alfalfa fields, on corn-silk
suits, or on a group of insane orangutans
who escaped from the St. Louis Zoo.
After Mack jumped into the cab
and stuffed his stash under the seat,
the orangutans scampered behind,
then hopped onto the tank, and got stuck
on metal hooks across the ceiling. They
started to screech, then threw banana debris
at a red Corvette whizzing by. Morgan
could take no more, so he flew out the door
and landed on the Corvette's floor,
where he still naps today.

QUEEN for a DAY

Bonita picks up quarters on the porch
of an empty house, one the locals claim
is haunted. She disagrees, crawls
on her knees, and breaks into the foyer,
responding to Julio's dare to spend a week
there—on her own. Then some toadstools
appear and make her feel weird about taking
up Julio's taunt. Soon Ralph the Baboon
hears of Bonita's doom, plops into his SUV
and roars into the yard. His truck runs
so loud, a neighbor phones the Coast Guard,
which arrives on the scene with AR-15s
they hoarded from the last war.

DERVISHES WHIRLING AGAIN

"Some people never go crazy.
What boring lives they must lead."
—Charles Bukowski

1

1 am Montauk. Rebecca Elizabeth,
an Indian Princess, born Ebonne,
Montauk Indian Tribe,
married Lt. Francis Bell, and
joined herself to the Brits here
in the states. After 12 generations
of begetting, those genes came to me.
But no father or mother,
grandfather or grandmother,
and so on up the tree
ever told me of this heritage.
So 1 became invisible, too.

2

According to some history books,
the Indigenous peoples kept
the air clean—no fire retardants to
cause mesothelioma, no asphalt roads,
no burning coal, no factories
spraying the atmosphere
with carbon monoxide.
And on and on.

3

Like graffiti on subway corridors,
the Pueblo painted bison and other
beasts on their cliff dwelling walls
in the Southwest. Was this the first
North American art apart from some
crashed Viking ships along Northeastern
Shores? Or were the Montauk
our first New York Artists
to display work outside
of galleries?

STARRY NIGHT ABOVE BLACK WATER

It was one of those days when Julio
felt lower than a grave till he watched a one-
legged man limp with a cane across the parking
lot. Though Julio wanted to write him love letters,
he thought it'd be better to write poems about
erotic crocs, enigmatic iguanas, and girls in pink hats
that look like duck buttocks. To bring Julio out of his
funk, Bonita appeared with her endearing elephant
earrings she'd inserted for his amusement. The two
escaped in a jeep Bonita picked up on the cheap,
and they circled Green Lake in the Rockies for hours.
Skies were so bright there—with Orion shooting his
arrows and spears, they quit caring about the Congress
that sent them grave-digging that morn.

SELF-PORTRAIT
as a Mailbox

Red, white, and blue—no svelte limbs,
I've little to do but hang out in this yard
for some action. A mailbox can't be picky.

I appeared overnight, and now, a man
who walks his Chihuahua every AM
stops and stares. He punches in 9-1-1.

The police arrive and shine flashlights
into my slot, perhaps to glean why
I'm inside a yard. My eyes glint red,

but I refrain from yapping or snapping.
Instead, I hold my breath. "No breathing,"
one says and phones animal control.

CASHING A CHECK

It was like this: Isabel didn't know where to buy food
for Wanda her iguana, the one her sister gave her
for Christmas last year. So she headed to Pike's
Peak where she figured she'd hit a streak of good
luck because the sun shone mightily, and her Chevy
pickup bucked and leapt over sand dunes on the way.
Then she skidded into a mudslide where Harold
the Asp hid. This woke him, and he chased Wanda
the Iguana across the plain. Isabel downshifted
to third and pondered how absurd this race had become.
She shimmied to the right, wiggled past Harold
and the saline-blighted stream, far from mean Jimmy
Blowfish who bullies minnows. She found Joe's Bait
Shop and stopped to buy Wanda's lunch,
cashing a check she hoped would pay the tab.

CASHING CHECKS

Juan won't ride with Isabel, even if he
finds cashing checks far more fun
than slinging his debit card. He keeps
track of checks better than cash,
especially when Willie the Giraffe hits him
up for a loan each time Juan roams the credit
union—or the ATM at the corner Drug Mart.
So today, checkbook in hand, he buzzes
by the Foothills, then onto Highway 82, and
rumbles to Lake Wallowa by way of Joseph,
Oregon. Who should appear there but
Jim Morrison in his full-leather gear. He asks
Juan to join him for a beer, but Juan says "not
today," and floats along, singing songs so
wrong, sparrows zoom by and bomb his
windshield. After those attacks, on the way
back, he stops to clean the glass at a Chevron
in Lostine. But the clerk there is so mean,
she screams, "No public johns!" Juan powers on,
but vows never to spin this way again, and he
writes checks all the way home.

TANKA STRINGS to KEEP IT TOGETHER, ESPECIALLY DURING a PANDEMIC

TROLLING THE KELP HIGHWAY*

Some scientists say
the first settlers came by sea—
followed Pacific
coastline reeds growing in sand,
before the Clovis trekked trails

on the Bering Strait
land-bridge across the ocean.
Archeologists
offer no snapshots of
unknown, pre-Clovis settlers

and stay mute about
whether they were explorers,
or if coastal trips
were all evacuations—
prehistoric trails of tears.

---

*Many scholars now support the "Kelp
Highway hypothesis" that the first settlers
in the Americas arrived after glaciers ebbed
from the Pacific Northwest coast about
17,000 years ago.

A PENGUIN'S TAKE on the UNIVERSE

*"Reality is merely an illusion,
albeit a very persistent one."*
—Albert Einstein

Not just black and white:
A man and woman skate—glide,
leap over a log
caught like some prehistoric
dinosaur or a gnome who

broke through ice too thin
and fell-in halfway. Its tail's
now wedged between two
worlds, like those of us who've trekked
the earth long enough to learn

it turns upside-down
in that instant when too few heed
those constellations
that help us navigate ice
flows and lead us home each night.

JIM ASKS, "WHERE'S ROBESPIERRE WHEN WE NEED HIM?"

> *"We must smother the internal and external*
> *enemies of the Republic or perish with it."*
> —M. Robespierre, *"On the Moral and*
> *Political Principles of Domestic Policy" (1794)*

> *"It was then the iguanas came."*
> —Louisa du Monde

Attacking lizards
left us powerless—as a
rowboat without oars—
a sprig of wheat in a field
turning mauve in a hailstorm,

a poem too frail
to open its fragile wings,
even in the sun,
after it's gained strength to face
another alligator.

TOO MUCH RELIANCE
on SCIENCE

"Reality is merely an illusion,
albeit a very persistent one."
—Albert Einstein

We are mere water.
Mutable fluids, we flow
then dribble ourselves
into visions of angels—
sightings of what may exist

or may not be there.
Solomon sips wine. The Queen
of Sheba studies
his face and asks to see gold,
jasper, lapis lazuli,

a millennium
of treasure to validate
his renowned wisdom.
Then effervescent bubbles
appear—an antique goblet

reflects another
mirror, and we stroll Versailles
hallways. A carriage
reminds us we are now with
Louis the XIV—no need

to lose our heads yet,
the guillotine comes after
we leave this era,
flow again to another
dimension far from the earth.

SELF-PORTRAIT: *Lizard*
near Coronado Heights

(Five Tankas)

Pale green, l flicker
my tongue, scurry through yuccas
wild grass, and sage brush.
My three-chambered heart beats
at 100 degrees, yet

I do not collapse,
do not hide under a rock,
don't crawl into holes,
but bask on sunlit clay plains
and inhale arid heatwaves.

Then the slow river
trickling through the desert
circles around rock
and sunny spot where l, Green
Lizard, stop and spread my claws.

Above, a red hawk
lifts red wings and maroon beak.
Underneath her breast,
she unfolds her coral feet
and lands near Green Lizard's seat.

Through the dying heat,
deep purple shadows encase
we creatures lying
on black rock rimmed with amber
edges—suspicions now gone.

JIM MORRISON and I LOSE OUR WAY on a MOON DOG NIGHT

The drive home's always
this way—too long, when sudden
changes shake us up.
After a few warm, sunny
days, cold winds hit us again.

Tonight, an odd haze
encircles the moon like white
light in an X-ray
outlining a frail hip bone
fallen into necrosis.

JIM and I WATCH NEW YORK NEWS:
A Steer Loose in Brooklyn

A Brahma wanders
streets, as if lost in traffic
he can't maneuver—
even though he made a quick,
clean slaughter-house breakaway.

Someone calls the cops.
They arrive in five squad cars.
Ambulance lights flare,
scare the steer till he charges
the whirling red discs. You ask,

"Where are the cowboys
when you need them? At least, where
are the mounted cops?"
"Usually, it's a lion,"
one says, "easier to catch."

I WATCH JIM
FIND a FOSSIL

for Anne Dvorak

Faded sand shifting—
millennia pressed into
striated layers,
eons of sepia rock
in an angry compression.

Its shadows now blend
into lines of blackened cliffs,
where dinosaurs roamed,
and saber-tooth tigers prowled,
their foot-long teeth piercing prey.

You find it today
in an archeology
shop, a museum
space not far from Pacific
coasts where your fossils remain.

SELF-PORTRAIT:
as the Earth

(*Rape Tankas*)

I say, "Stop." He says,
"So?" I say, "go." He says, "No,
no, no," and digs in,
unearthing iris, lilies,
and oaks with roots so locked-in

they won't ever free.
Cries still echo from the creek,
trickling into
Blue River, brown with debris.
Shadows of bare limbs flicker

and spread across dead
grass, parched from acid rain
hitting once again.
The chicken hawks roost and wait
for chipmunks who've given up.

SELF-PORTRAIT:
as the Ocean

five tankas for James Benger

I was once the sea.
Then, I blinked and saw fishes,
blue coral, breathing—
not locked inside some inlet
where currents can't be released.

Before I arrived,
The earth was formless and void.
Darkness filled waters.
God's Spirit whispered to waves,
"Let light be," and it was good.

Then God said, "Let space
separate ocean waters
from Heaven's waters,"
just as light separates night
from the radiance of day.

God named that space "sky"
and asked me to flow with seas
together as one.
So dry ground arose. The earth
He called "land" and oceans, "seas."

And he called for sprouts
to grow on the horizon,
fishes to fill seas—
Male, land, and female, ocean.
That's when the trouble began.

PERSEPHONE WARNS ME ABOUT JIM

(Five Tankas)

"Like your Jim," she says,
"Hades appeared magically
in the Field of Spring—
eternal spring—where I plucked
wildflowers for our new king.

"Other nymphs and I
selected perfect lilies,
smells sweet as iris,
white as we virgins—before
Hades arrived with sly words."

"Come with me," he said,
"live in my castle—far from
wind, rain, and hot sun.
You'll suffer no pain from Earth's
mercurial temperament."

"His words deceived me,"
she said, then lowered her eyes,
a tear glimmering
on each lid. "And I, Goddess
of Spring, now suffer winter—

eternally, see
Mother Demeter in spring
only. I hate life
in his hell, miss sunny days,
rue the day he seduced me."

IMMORTAL BELOVED—
Star-Crossed Once More

I search Pleiades
tonight, much like Ludwig sought
his beloved, a
star-crossed Romeo come too
late—Juliet departed

to another fate
without him. Like star showers,
they couldn't merge minds
but spread apart. Missing one
connection glimmering a

line to the north star,
they throb to one beat. We, too,
struggle for that link.
From our porch, we watch the skies
and wait until morning comes,

when we'll go at it
again—never win this fight.
Words out-of-kilter
fail to connect star wishes—
each horizon sinks them all.

LOST: *Great-Grandma's Pearl Earring*

(*Six Tankas*)

We jumped and *plié*-ed
outside the student center
on a cold day in
mid-December just before
Christmas Break my freshman year.

The pearls were real—not
cultured, Dad said and gave me
Great-grandma's earrings.
The gold, 18 karat, its
posts skewered, not like today's

cheap, slippery ones
molded from aluminum.
And yet, the post stripped,
slipped from my lobe to brown grass
in the lawn by the stone wall.

Gone, forever, like
Great-grandma and now, Father—
lost in onyx nights
that clutch me in their shadows
blinding me from spotting a

pearl hiding within
soil too gritty to unearth
when I need to keep
my hands immaculate, nails
pristine to finish my work.

I never found it—
that earring. I buried its
mate in my purse till
I moved it to a box with
photos of Dad and Nana.

SELF-PORTRAIT of
an AUTHOR IN SEARCH
of a THEME

"Rag and bone," Jim says,
repeating that line from Yeats.
I need more, and my
mind reels with why my uncle
killed himself after success,

not just with money,
but with a legal career
and respect from peers.
Corporate ills and Nero's
Sunken City undid him.

JIM MORRISON and I
SHARE SECRETS INSIDE a DINER

Red-roof, single-wide,
décor as if '65,
no lords and creatures
here, where Gus the cook offers
baseball stats 40 years back.

Fat sizzles on tin,
and we press our foreheads close
together as if
we're conspirators planning
our break in this shady spot

not far from LA.
I bite into a Sloppy
Joe, tap fingernails
on a Formica counter,
and stare at a cockatiel

calendar hanging
above yellow curtains that
embrace a window
framing a desert landscape
inviting us to escape.

"We must fly," Jim says,
"become the sky—erase past
memories that make
us weak—caught in caravans
wading through bloody corpses."

A red bush outside
teases me, and I, too, want
freedom from hunger
that drives us on scented winds,
while we squint through blurred windshields.

JIM and I STUDY CARAVAGGIO'S
ST. JOHN the BAPTIST

Nelson-Atkins Art Museum, Kansas City, Missouri

We stare at St. John
again. Rose and incense scents
seep into the room
while we watch black chasing white
in a chiaroscuro dance.

Michelangelo
Caravaggio was like
Jim—a wild spirit
who found little peace in life.
Yet his art lives forever,

as Jim's lyrics do.
The red cloth swaddling John—
passion in Jim's songs—
searching love on highways black
as leaves circling John's head.

A Nelson window
grows white as snow fills its ledge.
We fear black ice hides
in shoulders of highways we
must travel forever west

in our long journey
far from where we thumb pages
in art volumes here.
We'll peruse them more often,
we vow, after we ride home.

REFLECTIONS
(UPON JIM MORRISON'S RETURN)

COMIN' BACK to ME

The dawn inhales and holds its breath, drawing
wisps of clouds up the foothills, where they hover.
Jim steps out of the mist, unsteady as some soldier

searching for his platoon on a surreal battlefield.
He wedges boot heels into fissures between rock
ledges, ambles down to where gravel meets asphalt.

Then he steps onto the road leading to my Dutch
Colonel on a corner in this mountain college town,
where I chose to spend many of my remaining days,

watching parades of seasons pass in the hills'
kaleidoscope of colors revolving—in fall, scarlet,
gold, and bronze. In winter, cobalt blue and white.

Spring brings a rushed array—one week yellow,
the next red, then purple, and green never leaves
till late August, just before the aspen twitter

with orange and gold coins glittering in sunlight.
I don't see a move to Kansas or any spot east, wonder
if Jim and I will land in Venice, his California beach.

He raises a hand and yells, 'lo," his voice echoing
down to the street, falling at my knees, now trembling.
When he heads my way, I smell his Jade East, see

his hazy body morph into a solid physique, black
leather pants, jacket, and sandaled feet. He lifts his chin,
shakes his curls, then lowers his face and stares at me.

Still trembling, I remember our jaunts on a motorcycle
and a persnickety jeep—wonder if I'll ever be free again
or if I'll ride highways like some banshee for eternity.

STILL RIDING on the STORM

l figured he'd stay in the grave at Père-Lachaise,
near that spot in the thick shade where we parted.

But no. He still won't leave me alone. He hops
into view—not only when l hear one of his tunes,

but he slips in behind me, runs his fingertips
down my neck on those nights when l can't sleep.

The sweet throbs of those riders storming the crests
of thunder cracking on keyboards while Jim

warbles refrains sweet as kisses, sends tingles down
my spine and through ribs again, till I'm hooked

and can't help but take another look at the specter—
this phantom drifting in under my skin.

He won't leave me in peace until l sing and write
the words that free me from this space on earth

in these days of the pandemic—this virus killing
thousands more than the U.S. lost in its second

World War, far more than our nation saw lost
in Vietnam. And the marches have returned, too,

much like they were in the days Jim sang on stages
and let a shaman possess him like he has tonight.

JIM MORRISON and I
STOP BY VENICE BEACH

Tiny thing, this beach,
where Jim writes on a rooftop,
"Let's swim to the moon/
Let's climb through the tide,"*
and sings about a Crawling King Snake.

Sea winds circle us,
wrap us in thick mist
smelling of seaweed.
Haze hides the other side's rocks
We swim to them anyway.

Then we scurry up paths
trembling through cliffs and ledges,
far from family and friends—
back to the rooftop,
where Jim holds me captive.

---

*THE AMERICAN NIGHT. The Writings of Jim Morrison, Vol. II.
Random House/Vintage Books Edition, 1991, p. 97.

JIM and I ENCOUNTER a GHOST
at ST. JAMES HOTEL

Cimarron, New Mexico

Even if no breeze flows here—windows shut,
the lobby chandelier swings back and forth
in an incessant rhythm as if someone shoved it.
I smell spicy incense from the Orient,
and the guide says a ghost haunts Room 118.

It's the 1881 card player, she adds. He won the hotel
in Five-card stud but was shot before he cashed in.
Then, there!—in a shadowy corner, a transparent
poker player studies his hand. He glances
up when Jim and I step inside the parlor.

Hotel namesake St. James the Greater, a martyr
under Herod Agrippa, was the son of Zebedee
and brother to St. John. He was the older apostle
named James. Jesus gave him and John
the surname, *Boanerges*—

"Sons of Thunder"—for their fiery tempers.
Yet, only they and Peter witnessed His transfiguration.
I wonder why the gambler ghost doesn't join St. James
in the light—bright enough to show a winning hand—
to win a place no bullet can steal.

THE GHOST of SPECIAL NEEDS

for Jim Morrison
at Rancho de Taos, New Mexico

You wait outside the adobe church,
its thick, mauve walls built
more than three centuries back.
I asked you to join me,
but you refuse to enter

this holy spot where I genuflect,
slide into a pew, and sing
Spanish love songs to God
with Pueblo and Hispanic
parishioners. We clap our hands,

while you wait in the SUV,
looking more a suburbanite
dad than the Lizard King
you claim to be. Not me.
When I sing here, I'm free.

No one pays attention
to whether I sing on key—
or if I miss a lyric or two
when I hum through a few
in "Nearer my God to Thee."

JIM and I TRUDGE
to ST. MARK'S

Colwich, Kansas

The old fire stones lie cold
and alone in the shade
of the steeple at St. Mark's
Cathedral, whose bell tower
overlooks grasslands.
We try to climb the hill
where it stands, but stop
too often to catch our breath.

FDR understood how hard
it is to move forward
when dragging a leg, like me.
And soon, we must escape
this place where thick air
clogs nostrils, makes inhaling
a chore with every step
uphill on a humid day.

Jim stops, squats under an oak,
and I slide in beside him.
"St. Mark wrote my favorite
gospel," he says. "He minced
no words—just told the straight
story. His form is an angel
of soul." I reply, "I know."
I don't say I like John's best.

PASTURE SCENE: JIM and I
WAKE NEAR the FLINT HILLS

> *"A quavering*
> *column of coyote song rises to the sky. . ."*
> *—Steven Hind, "Waking in the Flint Hills"*

Not far from the Verdigris River,
Jim yawns and wriggles out
of the sleeping bag we share.
We watch a deer crouch
to give birth in a shaded field,
close to the river bank,
where we lodged last night.

Diesels roar down the highway
as they've done since before
Steven penned his words,
crows pick at roadkill
for breakfast, and we hear
the grasses whine
backup for a song

Jim hums as he pulls
out his canteen.
Then a coyote sings another
melody from red bluffs
on the horizon—we smell
bluestem and try to avoid
the lyrics that mirror our lives.

JIM MORRISON and I HUNT GHOSTS in ELLINWOOD, KANSAS

The Historic Wolf Hotel

We speed on hot coffee—black as asphalt on Kansas
      Route 56—and we push on.
An orange moon smears the horizon, leaves a sparkling
      road trail.

We buzz past dry wheat fields into Ellinwood, to the
      Historic Wolf Hotel.
There, Miss Sally, the resident ghost, lives. We don't see her
      but hear soft beats

and sweet guitar riffs from Simon and Garfunkel tunes.
      Music and red Vette
at the curb tell me it's 1965, six years before Jim died.
      Tonight, we're alive.

No ambulance clangs on Boulevard Street or idles in a drive.
No choppers hover over asphalt. No sirens shriek
      like the time

firemen lugged me on a gurney, chest bleeding, into the ER.
They shoved a tube into my side to plump a lung collapsed

from a hunting knife jabbed at my heart. Later,
nurses slap me in a bed, and rivet me to a wall.

No smells of alcohol and anesthetics dry my nostrils.
No bustling like the night I arrived broken—aching

and Jim no longer drools saliva after a night of booze
      and needles.
No bathtub waits for him to slide into while his head's
      not straight.

JIM MORRISON and I HANG OUT in the UPTOWN ARTS BAR

Kansas City, Missouri

We slide into seats at a dark
table near the bar, and Jim reads
from Blake's poem, "The Marriage
of Heaven and Hell": "The road
of excess leads to the palace of wisdom."
He glances at me and adds,
"So we must push through
the doors of perception,
go another direction.
Then we'll reach heaven."

I listen but squint at the steep,
white, crown molding
parading scalloped sashes
that circle the ceiling
over the bar. To the right,
a huge red and black
abstract—almost a Miro
painting with bold strokes
and thick paint—returns
me to this century.

I wonder how Jim sees such visions
in this bar, where I watch men
who dress like women, wearing
long hair teased high
into bouffant styles.
In tight, black skirts slit to thighs,
they shimmy across the floor,
and wait tables of drunks
who sometimes squeeze buttocks
and pinch their false tits.

JIM and I WATCH the WINDMILLS of WESTERN KANSAS

Like roods with revolving crossbars,
they line the flat horizon, roll on and on—
Grateful Dead concerts
tumbling through riffs that morph
into different melodies before we know
our minds start flowing there—far beyond

Kansas and its flat pastures
that seem to never end, except
through the Flint Hills—but then,
they flow back into plains,
now mauve in the western sun.
And more windmills churn on

atop a round horizon
of brown-gold bluffs interlaced
with the green Northwest brush.
Its verdant hue lets us know
Kansas isn't far enough away
from the traffic we want to escape.

SHAMAN BLUES ROCKER

(one more Jim Morrison dance)

Jim's at it again, moving like a snake
or rooster—I'm unsure which.
Shaman-dancing to a blues beat,
he sings "love comes in familiar
faces," and "love comes
to those who seek it."

But when I've loved men wild
as Jim, each leaves me bleeding.
No matter how I scrub love's
stains from my skin,
they won't go away.
No bleach works.

Now the music's over. Jim dances
and hears the butterfly's scream,
away from the crowds,
away from cameras,
away from cops who find glory
in locking him away.

JIM MORRISON and I HEAD to STANDING ROCK

Dakota Pipeline, North Dakota

When clouds form an eagle above a red sun,
and the Flint Hills and dried-up wheat fields
beckon us onward, we head east and north—

beyond the Great Plains and the narrow lanes
to which we'd become accustomed—after spinning
across sand in our chase for California dreams

of peace and love, still uncaptured. Here, police
shoot pepper spray and water cannons at 30 of us.
Security guards unleash dogs that maim six,

one a small child. Still, we clutch signs—black
crosses against a blue sky, where cirrus clouds
hover then become black knots of rain.

We clasp hands with the Standing Rock Sioux,
pray with them in a circle, and I ask Jim
if he wants to risk getting arrested.

He shakes his head. "We'll help. But this is their
Wounded Knee. It isn't to be fought by you—by me."
He pulls out three fifties to leave for munitions.

I nod to agree, it's the natives' call. Even if it's for all
of us, they must win it in these unaligned times
when the eagle cloud rises high on the horizon.

I TELL JIM of MY MONTAUK HERITAGE

"You never lived as a second class citizen,"
he said, "you passed on white privilege—"

Even if true, Jim's words still stung sharply
as a stiletto wound. My pale skin may "pass,"

but I feel pain akin to those on the Rez, eating
haphazard meals, canned corn and beans.

Even if I lived in a White-bread suburb,
old wagons were all Mother could afford.

And collecting toys is a hard board game
to win when you're one of seven children.

So I painted and read, grew a life from books—
Austin's novels and Twain's *Huckleberry Finn*,

and those shows now airing on Cozy TV—
those sit-coms touting suburban families—

comedies conning us to drop our cash on
studded jeans, Mustangs, Corvettes, and MGs.

Those TV parents didn't swat kids or yell, not
like the hell I'd seen, much akin to the Rez scene.

I glare at Jim and squint. "Don't say mean words.
You don't know what it's like being me."

JIM'S LAUGHTER FRIGHTENS ME

He squints at Lost Lake,
stares and blinks a tear, as if
it were the Pacific, where
he'd morph into vapor
and merge with ocean mists.
"The Lords are within us,"
he says. His laughter
echoes so loud, it sets nearby
cottonwoods trembling.

"The Lords within us are born
of sloth and cowardice,"*
he yells, flails his arms,
and runs toward the lake.
Smelling of mildew,
heavy fog hovers
and clogs our nostrils.
I inhale it and cough. Still,
I follow Jim into the waves.

"I tell you this." He laughs again.
I tremble when he adds, "No
eternal reward will forgive us
for wasting the dawn."**
Then he dips his fedora
into water, lifts it high,
and pours it over my head.
I wonder what baptism
this is—and if I can follow him.

---

*Jim Morrison. *THE LORDS and THE NEW CREATURES: Poems.*
    Simon & Schuster/A Touchstone Book, 1969 (paper 2012, p. 104).

**THE AMERICAN NIGHT. *The Writings of Jim Morrison,* Vol. II.
    Random House/Vintage Books Edition, 1991, p. 126.

JIM MORRISON TELLS ME I HAVE GREEK FEET

Jim claims inherited feet shapes
are based on their origins.
"With that index toe outgrowing
your hallux (big toe)," he says,
"yours are Greek." Then he grins.

For decades, I ignored my feet,
except to clean—soak in Epson salts—
until this year, when they bleed.
I rub a pumice stone over cracks,
wait for them to heal, and
meditate about feet:
Cornerstones to columns,
pedestals to pillars—
our feet hold up our worlds.

Greek feet—barefoot runners
leap across urns for eternity.
Greeks used few feet in poetry—
Sappho's many lines lost.
And they wrote plays
in couplets, repeating the first line's
number of feet in the next,
so back-row listeners knew
who spoke when feet repeated.

"You know that means you dominate
a marriage or household," Jim adds,
grins again, wrinkles his nose.
"I don't," I boldly say.
"I am still waiting for that to be."

ERASURES

Some one's erasing my life—
the bungalow where I was born.
The château where I birthed my daughter.
The Cape Cod where I raised my son—
all gone.

Turquoise ponds we skinny dipped,
hot clay shores where we unearthed clams.
No more. Only hot winds there—
no more cattails and cottages or cows
roaming free.

No map shows the cabins on the lake
where we boated and water skied,
as if our lives would roll on and on—
No more willows, waters on shores, ebbing
and flowing.

Jim and I howl at the moon, then slip away—
follow shadows into black spaces.
We're lunatics who've lost direction,
spinning like my cat with an aneurism—
also gone.

And They expect us to march uphill,
act courageous about our futures—
winners of a nation—when They
block out our victories, our memories,
our past.

OUR NANTUCKET in the FOOTHILLS

Quite far from Nantucket,
we set up our estate—
not as plush as the summer palace
of Jackie Kennedy Onassis.
Her daughter Caroline put it on the market:
$65 million for the estate Ari bought in 1979
and used for family escapes, days hidden
by Martha's Vineyard in Aquinnah.

On the opposite side of this continent,
we hide in the foothills and a college
town—Northeast Oregon.
Our historic house was built
in 1906, a Dutch colonial
with a barn-shaped roof.
Eccentric perhaps—a match
for us, two poets with thin roots.
From our front window, we
watch each season cross the foothills,
bringing wind, snow, mountain flowers,
green, then gold bluffs,

unlike the Onassis clan, who watched
the Atlantic's rolling, cold waves
from almost every window,
saw their hopes and wishes
washing to shore—fishes running
aground, going astray.

NO MORE CASHING CHECKS?

It isn't as if I've always been flush with cash—
and Jim's known for burning his like autumn leaves.

Still, we believed we'd cash our checks
when they arrived. Yet today, some banks may

contrive other plans. It's scary. *The Atlantic*
claims we're moving away from paper money.

I worry about days when there won't be any
checks to cash. Or when bitcoins take over.

A politician yaks about making this nation "great again,"
as if he'd never learned about equivocating words.

Then he returned our world into another Great Depression,
with a Gilded Age pandemic—that he ignored

and refused to prepare for. So today, instead of being
paid with fresh cash or a solid check we could wrap

our fists around, inhale crisp smells of Jefferson's
face—or perhaps Grant's on a larger amount,

we receive pay electronically or on a SNAP card
so we can pay taxes and eat. Either way, it isn't

sweet as the meat we receive when we exchange
checks for the sweet green life we know—

and when we can share passing along cash,
check our fears and remorse at the door.

ACKNOWLEDGMENTS

"After Reading 'Saudade' by Erika L. Sánchez" (*Thorny Locust* 2018).

"Antigone's Rant" (*Flint Hills Review* 2018).

"Self-Portrait as Bathsheba" (Library Webpage, Blue Mountain Community College Spring 2019). (Runner-up in Pendleton Warming Center Contest).

"Self-Portrait in Cracked Mirror" (*Thorny Locust* 2019).

"Persephone Waits at the Hades Intersection" (*Flint Hills Review* 2018).

"No Exit" (*365 Days: A Poetry Anthology* Vol. 3 2020)

"Relativity Lesson," (*The Shining Years: An Anthology about Aging* 2020).

"Ashe's People" (*365 Days: A Poetry Anthology* Vol. 3 2020).

"Day of the Dead" (revised from "Re-reading 'The Second Coming' by W.B. Yeats"), *Where Water Meets the Rock* (39 WEST Press 2017), (also in *The Enigmatist* 2017).

"Quantum Mechanical Love" (*Thorny Locust* 2017).

"Self-Portrait as Second Wife" (*I-70 Review* 2019).

"Kohl-rimmed Eyes" (*Ekphrastic Review*, "Egyptian Challenge" February 2019).

"I Hear America Melting" (*365 DAYS: A Poetry Anthology* Vol. 2 2018).

"Along the Curb" (*365 DAYS: A Poetry Anthology* Vol. 2 2018).

"Mirror Images," (*The Shining Years: An Anthology about Aging* 2020).

"Narcissus in the Old Folks Home" (*I-70 Review* 2021)

"How You Dull the Pain under this Silent Canopy" from an earlier version, "Silent Canopy" in *Where Water Meets the Rock* (39 WEST PRESS 2017), (also in *Phantom Drift* 2017).

"A Mortal Leash" (*365 Days: A Poetry Anthology* Vol. 3 2020).

"My Front Door in the Time of the Corona" (*Silver Birch Press* May 2020)

"Black Hijab: My Mask" (*365 Days: A Poetry Anthology* Vol. 4 2021).

"Fox Soup II (Downtown Abbey)" from "Fox Soup" (*The Same* 2017).

"Cashing a Check" (*Thorny Locust* 2018).

"Trolling the Kelp Highway" (*365 DAYS: A Poetry Anthology* Vol. 2 2018).

"A Penguin's Take on the Universe" (*365 DAYS: A Poetry Anthology* Vol. 2 2018).

"Too Much Reliance on Science" (*365 DAYS: A Poetry Anthology* Vol. 2 2018).

"Self-Portrait: Lizard near Coronado Heights" (*Thorny Locust* 2019).

"Jim and I Watch New York News: A Steer Loose in Brooklyn," also known as "A Steer Loose in Brooklyn" (*Thorny Locust* 2018).

"Self-Portrait as the Ocean" (*365 DAYS: A Poetry Anthology* Vol. 3 2020.)

"LOST: Great-grandmother's Pearl Earring"
(*Silver Birch Press* March 2017).

"Jim Morrison and I Hunt Ghosts in Ellinwood, Kansas"
(*Thorny Locust* 2018).

"Jim Morrison and I Hang out in the Uptown Arts Bar"
(*Thorny Locust* 2017).

"Jim and I Watch the Windmills of Western Kansas" (also known
as "Windmills of Western Kansas" (*Thorny Locust* 2020),
(*Silver Birch Press* re-ran 2020).

"Jim Morrison and I Head to Standing Rock"
(*Silver Birch Press*, November 2021).
(Originally released in *Tittynope Zine* Issue 2: 2017)

"Jim Morrison Tells Me I Have Greek Feet"
(*Silver Birch Press*, June 2021).

"Erasures" (*I-70 Review* 2020).

"Our Nantucket in the Foothills"
(*365 Days: A Poetry Anthology* Vol. 3 2020).

Although the author imagined most of Jim's words in this work,
some of them came from his writings:

Jim Morrison. *THE LORDS and THE NEW CREATURES: Poems.*
Simon & Schuster/A Touchstone Book, 1969 (paper 2012).

THE AMERICAN NIGHT. The Writings of Jim Morrison, Vol. II.
Random House, Inc./Vintage Books Edition, 1991.

The author also wants to thank Jerry Hopkins and Danny Sugerman
for the *Biography of JIM MORRISON: No One Here Gets Out
Alive*. Hachette Book Group, Inc./Grand Central Publishing,
1981, 1995, 2006.

ABOUT THE AUTHOR

PHOTO BY NELLI SUDBROCK

Lindsey Martin-Bowen's fourth poetry collection, *Where Water Meets the Rock* was nominated for a Pulitzer Prize, her third, *CROSSING KANSAS with Jim Morrison* (in chapbook form) was a semi-finalist in the QuillsEdge Press 2015–2016 Chapbook Contest. In 2017, it won the Kansas Writers Association award, "Looks Like a Million." In 2016, *Writer's Digest* gave her "Vegetable Linguistics" an Honorable Mention in its 85th Annual Contest (Non-rhyming Poetry Category). Her *Inside Virgil's Garage* (Chatter House Press 2013) was a runner-up in the 2015 Nelson Poetry Book Award, and a poem from that collection was nominated for a Pushcart Prize. McClatchy Newspapers named her *Standing on the Edge of the World* (Woodley Press/ Washburn University) one of the Ten Top Poetry Books of 2008. It was nominated for a Pen Award.

Her poems have run in *New Letters*, *I-70 Review*, *Thorny Locust*, *Tittynope Zine*, *Coal City Review*, *Amethyst Arsenic*, *Silver Birch Press*, *Flint Hills Review*, *Bare Root Review*, *The Same*, *Phantom Drift*, *Porter Gulch Review*, *Rockhurst Review*, 21 anthologies, and other literary magazines. She taught at the University of Missouri-Kansas City 18 years and often concurrently at MCC-Longview 25 years, and now she teaches writing, Criminal Law, Criminal Procedure, and American Court Systems and Practices (online) for Blue Mountain Community College in Pendleton, Oregon. She holds an MA from the University of Missouri and a *Juris Doctor* degree from the UMKC Law School.

In a previous life, she was a full-time newspaper reporter for *The Louisville Times* (Louisville, Colorado) and for The *SUN* Newspapers (Johnson County, Kansas), an associate editor for *Modern Jeweler Magazine* and the editor for *The National Paralegal Reporter*.

For other titles available from redbat books, please visit:
www.redbatbooks.com

Also available through Ingram, Bookshop.org,
Amazon.com, Powells.com and by special order
through your local bookstore.

www.ingramcontent.com/pod-product-compliance
Lightning Source LLC
Chambersburg PA
CBHW031144090426
42738CB00008B/1209

9 781946 970091